AF215290

Mantram
Beach

~

ARUN KUMAR

ALEPH

ALEPH

ALEPH BOOK COMPANY
An independent publishing firm
promoted by *Rupa Publications India*

First published in India in 2020 by
Aleph Book Company
7/16 Ansari Road, Daryaganj
New Delhi 110002

ISBN: 978-81-947353-5-9

1 3 5 7 9 10 8 6 4 2

Printed at Replika Press Pvt. Ltd, India.

For Poornima

CONTENTS

NATURAL FORCES

STORIES OF PEOPLE

Home and the World

VISITING THE OLD HOMETOWN

Each avenue is a remembered year,
The one by the hospital where two sons were born,
Then the road to the elementary school,
Where they dived behind the bushes
To avoid the little angels who chased them at Halloween,
Makes a right angle with the street
Leading to the high school of robotics competitions.
The varsity soccer fields abutting El Camino Real
Speak of victories and defeats,
Other streets, of years of visits to dentists and paediatricians.
On campus, the path to university events and convocations
Sees graduate students who will one day
Incorporate time and memory into spatial maps.

MANTRAM BEACH

Walking this crescent of sand ringed by the cliffs of Marin,
Easwaran and Christine, seekers from the East and the West,
Whispered seers' secrets to a thirsty Pacific:

Words from Krishna, Gautama, Christ, St Francis of Assisi,
Words to penetrate the fogs of the mind's confusion,
Words with the fresnel focus of the headland lighthouses.

Walk this crescent chanting a mantram of Shiva,
Let the rhythmic ocean salve the suffering mind,
Let the cold water, the cold winds cleanse you:

Waves that erase footprints and follies,
Waves that carry the wisdom of the past and present,
Waves that fill every interstice of your being.

Chidaananda roopah, shivoham shivoham.

FAMILY TEMPLE
(for Shaila)

Driving through relentless rain as the day dimmed,
An impromptu detour brought us to our ancient
family temple.

The leaking sky attempted to douse the lightning
That intermittently lit the alleyway to our destination.

Wading through the darkness, drenched,
We entered, refugees from the storm,

Into a serene sanctuary, oblivious of tumult.
A kindly priest sat alone, performing an ancient ritual

For a goddess bedecked in silk and adorned with
sandal paste,
Who seemed to smile beatifically to bless,

While he averted his attention briefly towards us,
With a benign nod of acknowledgement.

SHWEDAGON PAGODA

Below the golden spire pointed to heaven,
A timeless tranquillity transcends
The frenetically changing colours
Of LED haloes and exploding stars
Lighting the faces of Buddhas
In classic postures of blessing.
Languid young mendicants, saffron-clad,
Snap selfies, starting their reflexive journeys,
Sharing instantly over social media.

JOURNEY
(for Amartya Zaran)

Travelling across the country to see my grandson,
Delayed in Chicago airport on Christmas Eve,
A pause forced by midwestern storms,
I sit back to view a passing show of passengers
Aiming to unite with parents, grandparents, siblings;
A father tries to amuse his year-old son.

Christmas-time journeys began two thousand years ago,
Melchior, Balthasar, and Gaspar were guided by a star
To Bethlehem, bearing gold, frankincense, and myrrh.
Our transits are faster now, guided by satellite navigation,
And self-willed stars will not find new ways, and yet
Our stories will always be about journeys.

ENGLISH ESTANCIA

Whipped by gusts from the ice fields,
At the centre of a vast dish of low grassland
Rimmed by the snow-topped serrations of the cordillera,
The English estancia stands.

It shuts itself off with a protective shield
Of birch trees, a circle around its self-selected solitude,
As myriad acres of grasses
Roll like waves in the Patagonian wind.

Within: a row of roses, a tended lawn,
A kitchen garden as in the old country,
A yearning to slip this expanse
For an imagined life, a long-ago homeland.

SAMARKAND

The colour of Samarkand is not red.
There is no sign of the blood that flowed
When Alexander, Genghis, and Timur
Captured this jewel set in blue and gold.

The sound of Samarkand is silence.

No fierce footfalls of charging horses,
No spears clanking nor soldiers screaming.
Instead, the quiet walks of visitors,
Camera clicks, inaudible sighs.

UTAWALA, NAIROBI

Away from the gleaming city centre,
Where chic brand names line posh streets,
Names that proclaim superiority and premium prices
Confidently asserted in swank cities around the world,

This nondescript suburb hosts humble stores
With names that are earnest, reaching into the core
Of human yearning, for gifts sought that have no price:
Blessing Grocery, Mercy Electronics, and the Ultimate
Hair Salon.

LET SPELLING BE

In how many ways can you spell shop?
Stores aspiring to quaintness use shoppe
As in Old Curiosity. But who can improve
On Lucky Feng Shui Shoppy?

In how many ways can you spell omelette?
In America, they prefer omelet.
The transcendentals prefer aumlet
But my Mumbai menu says aumletty.

Animal Spirits

PARTY ANIMALS

Observe them, the novelist says,
Sipping her Chardonnay,
Can you name the species?

See how they move
In the genteel jungle
Of the cocktail party.

Watch the preeners,
The cockerels, strutting
With a touch of colour.

Note the predator eyes
Of interlocutors hunting
For elusive prey,

The lissome cheetahs,
Lions and scented lionesses
Fluidly closing in.

And the jackals prowling
Behind the hunters to observe
And, post party, vivisect.

THE SHEARING

Roberto from the north,
Strong and silent,
Pulls her from the holding pen.

She resists, briefly, slightly,
While dragged into the arena
Where the tourist-voyeurs wait.

He lays her on her back,
Hapless feet upwards,
Her head between his thighs.

With an electric shear
He adroitly, rapidly,
Cuts away the wool,

Stripping her, systematically,
As her full teats come into view
In a public denuding.

Puzzled, slightly bruised,
Naked, she looks at us:
Have you seen enough?

He then throws the wool on the floor
With a flourish: expertly extracted
As a single piece, a dusty carpet

That washed, wool-sorted, dyed, spun, and knit
Will someday somewhere cover,
Tightly, another fulsome figure.

SERANGOON STREET SCENE

Wire cages imitating houses
With domes and arches,
Hold colourful budgerigars, parrots,
That peck and feed and sip.

Birds for a price.

Below them, the sparrows,
Brown, dusty, nondescript,
Dart to feed on grains
That drizzle from the cages.

Birds shooed away.

A sparrow flies up to a cage
Peers inside, curious
To observe the well-fed captives
Whose surplus feeds the free.

LIFE AND DEATH ON THE PAMPAS

Arranged on the bleached steppe, a biology lesson:
The neat blanched skeleton of a guanaco.
Around the scene, on the ridges of succeeding ranges,
Young guanaco stand, silhouetted sentinels,
Tasked by their herds to spot puma.
This one was not lucky,
The Patagonian wind dispersed the hostile scent.
Puma, and then condor, got to work.

SEARCHING FOR BORGES

In his city of streets laid out in grids,
Penetrated by radial roads like the spokes of a wheel
Coming off the Plaza San Martin,
There is one deviant avenue: Maipu.
It appears by the Plaza, briefly,
Then disappears.
To catch its flow, we switch back and forth,
Ask instructions in a language we do not know,
Check Google Maps which itself is confounded
By this street's caprice.
Any wonder this is where he chose to live?
He wrote of labyrinths and forking paths,
Conflated fact with fantasy, fame and infamy.
And then we find the plaque,
Teasingly off the Plaza, hiding
At the spot where we began our search:
Maipu 944, residence of Jorge Luis Borges.

KAMALA DAS GRAVE

Underground, unmarked,
She lies in official anonymity,
Under the spread of a mahogany tree,
In the grounds of the mosque.

She still makes a statement,
And still breaks the rules,
As two willowy green plants
Point to where she is interred.

LOCKDOWN

Outside the windows of my study,
The gulmohur rustles deep red flames,
Green parrots streak through clean air,
Sea breeze whispers from the Breach Candy shore,
While the blue curtain of a cloudless sky
Muffles sounds into an ominous silence.

A lethal agent, invisible, is abroad the earth,
Humans cower, suddenly bereft of power
As the malign mist of a mocking virus
Locks down cities, clears roads and skies.
As evening comes, the bats on the tree outside
Begin to stir, their dark wings flap...

Natural Forces

CHANGING SCENE

Each day they paint the sky:
Silhouetted cypresses on Land's End,
Slender swaying stalks, frond-brushes
That splash water-colour greys
On misty San Francisco mornings,
Then dip into the Pacific
To coat the sky a deep azure.
They rest while the advancing sun
Bleaches the blue lazily.
Post siesta, a palette of oils:
Arraying deep red, orange, yellow
In layers over shades of cerulean,
Flecks of white below as muffled breakers
Move against the cliff in concentric rhythm.

GUDALUR, NILGIRIS

As the mercury drops at nightfall,
The quick cover of night is interrupted;
An inexorable white saw cuts in half the grey-blue sky.
Thunder rumbles from the Mudumalai
And its animals cower.
Then, with morning, a cacophony of predation,
The sun rises from behind teak and bamboo;
Birds chirp away the remains of the night,
The dew dries out, and the bougainvillea
Light up in lilac and red.

USHUAIA

Mellow daylight accents colours of houses, flowers,
Then fades to grey as the long day ends
In this city of more vowels than consonants,
Its name a three-syllabic exhalation.

The earth spins slower here, as at the tip of a top,
Balancing, circus-like, two Americas, South and North,
While taming the turbulent Atlantic
To tippy-toe its way around the curves of the cordillera

Through the narrow Beagle Channel,
Past ships safe in harbour, with winking lights
And periodic horns announcing departure,
To find communion with the Pacific.

SNOW IN DETROIT

Downy white swirls
Climbed centrifugally
To my forty-second-floor window,
Then hovered over the river
To form a translucent curtain
Separating two countries,
Diffusing the winks
Of Windsor's casinos.

CENTRAL VALLEY, CALIFORNIA

Between the serrated Sierra and the jagged Coast Ranges,
Lies a carpet of squares and oblongs, shades of green, yellow,
A vast Mondrian outstretched,
Tinted by waterways that moisten the desert
While controlling the run-offs of turbulent rivers,
Defying nature's disorder with patterned geometries.

RED RIVER, FARGO

Our rivers run east, west, and south,
To mingle into large oceans.
But this one runs north!
Through the great flat plains of the midwest,
It darts its way through the prairie,
Imagining a sea somewhere up north,
But must settle for a lake.
In the winter, the north gets colder sooner,
The lake it has found freezes over,
Pushing back on the Red River
To spill into its very shallow valley
Forming a sea of its own,
Creating its desired destination.

THE OHIO

Most rivers meander.
They zig and zag lazily
Around obstacles
In no hurry to reach the sea.

But the Ohio does not wander.
She runs in straight lines
And makes purposive sharp turns,
Hastening to her destiny.

CALIFORNIA LIVE OAK

Untended, she will grow
Into a globe-like shrub,
Her myriad spiny convex leaves
Forming a shield to keep you out.

Tend her, shape her, guide her
To grow her branches long and high,
Creating an inviting shade below:
Cultivated appeal and gravitas.

Stories of People

ODE TO NICK
(for Nicholas Horsburgh)

Spirited and in his core, spiritual,
Scholar equally of Sanskrit and Senthamil,
Living the lessons of Sankara's advaita:
Preferring the one, the singular; the single malt
And soma are but manifestations
Of the same distillate, ethyl or ethereal...
The oneness of East and West
Lives through his laughter and love.

AUNG SAN SUU KYI

She glides, a slim and stately presence,
Across the marble floors
Of the new Parliament house
Alongside the strongman generals
Whose longyis muffle their military gait.
As we walk, she reminisces
Of her days in Delhi, and visits to Kerala.
Then, around the conference table,
Her elegance is prelude to eloquence,
But the jasmine in her hair is wilting.

REMEMBERING

When I sat silently by my eighty-year-old mother,
As she poured me tea

Or walked slowly with her around the seashore temple,
Early in the morning

Listening, as she took me back through the years
To when she was a little girl

The timelines and tumults of my world gave way
To a simpler time, a simple peace.

WEDDING

Standing by my son, doe-eyed, delicate,
She confidently accepted his ring
As her professor, officiating, explained
The tradition of the Vedic wedding.

Now, she is my son's wife,
A new daughter in our family.
How lucky we are, but how unfair—
What have we done to deserve her?

How dare we think she will be our daughter?
Who are we to lay any claim on her affection?
I must tell her mother and father
Their work is mostly done, ours has just begun.

WAITING
(for Vidur)

A hushed and cleaned-up earth awaits,
With blue skies yielded to the birds
That soar, while urban noise abates
On streets empty of human herds.

A new life in our human chain,
Now floating in a fluid sac,
Will soon emerge, and we will gain
Despite the pandemic—our mojo back!

NAMING

Surrounded by mother, grandmother, great-grandmother,
Father, grandfather, uncles, grand-uncles,
She is centre stage

At her naming ceremony, when her uncle whispers
Into one ear, then the other,
Her name

Now longer than she is, that she will grow into,
Multisyllabic, musical,
Mrinalini.

CAFÉ EL FISHAWY

In the din of the Khan el-Khalili,
Naguib Mahfouz quietly wrote,
Seeing the world through an apple-scented mist,
Sipping cups of perfumed tea.

The hookah's embers slow burned his plots,
Rising through a haze of bubbling fumes,
Accenting sights of love and loss
Of people milling in the marketplace.

LIFE'S ACCOUNTING

A student once, of Latin, Greek, the classics,
She expounds upon accounting methods
In terms fundamental, the basics

Of making smooth the closing process,
Of ageing accounts unreconciled,
Of measuring failure and success.

Outside, an eagle soars among skyscrapers
Lego-stacked against a deep blue sky,
Distracting me from her talk of ledgers…

The Bay Bridge spans azure waters,
The smooth hills of the Diablo range beyond.
But let's now focus on period-end matters

Ageing, reconciling, closing…

INDEX OF FIRST LINES

In the din of the Khan el-Khalili,   45

Mellow daylight accents colours of houses, flowers,   31

Most rivers meander.   35

Observe them, the novelist says,   17

Our rivers run east, west, and south,   34

Outside the windows of my study,   26

Roberto from the north,   19

She glides, a slim and stately presence,   40

Spirited and in his core, spiritual,   39

Standing by my son, doe-eyed, delicate,   42

Surrounded by mother, grandmother, great-grandmother,   44

The colour of Samarkand is not red.   11

Travelling across the country to see my grandson,   9

Underground, unmarked,   25

Untended, she will grow   36

Walking this crescent of sand ringed by the cliffs of Marin,   4